Bread

Dedication
For my young son William who is just
discovering the joys of breadmaking.

A Pyramid Paperback

First published in Great Britain in 2007 by
Hamlyn, a division of Octopus Publishing Group Ltd,
2–4 Heron Quays, London E14 4JP

The recipes in this book were previously published in
The Bread Book, by Hamlyn

ISBN-13: 978-0-600-61603-0
ISBN-10: 0-600-61603-7

A CIP catalogue record for this book is available from the
British Library

Printed and bound in China

10 9 8 7 6 5 4 3 2 1